STECK-

NEW WAY

HEADS and TAILS

Glad or Sad?

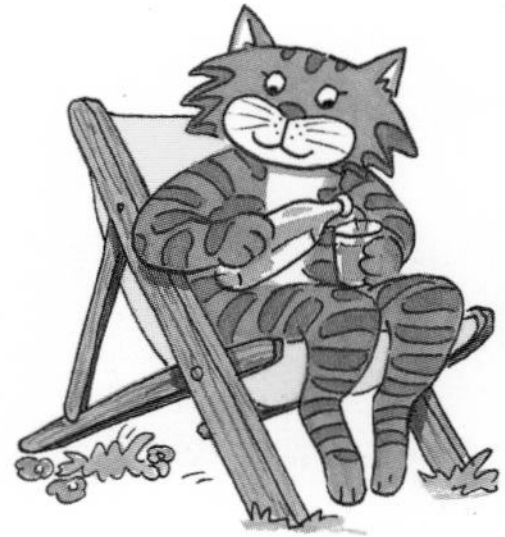

STECK-VAUGHN COMPANY

A Division of Harcourt Brace & Company

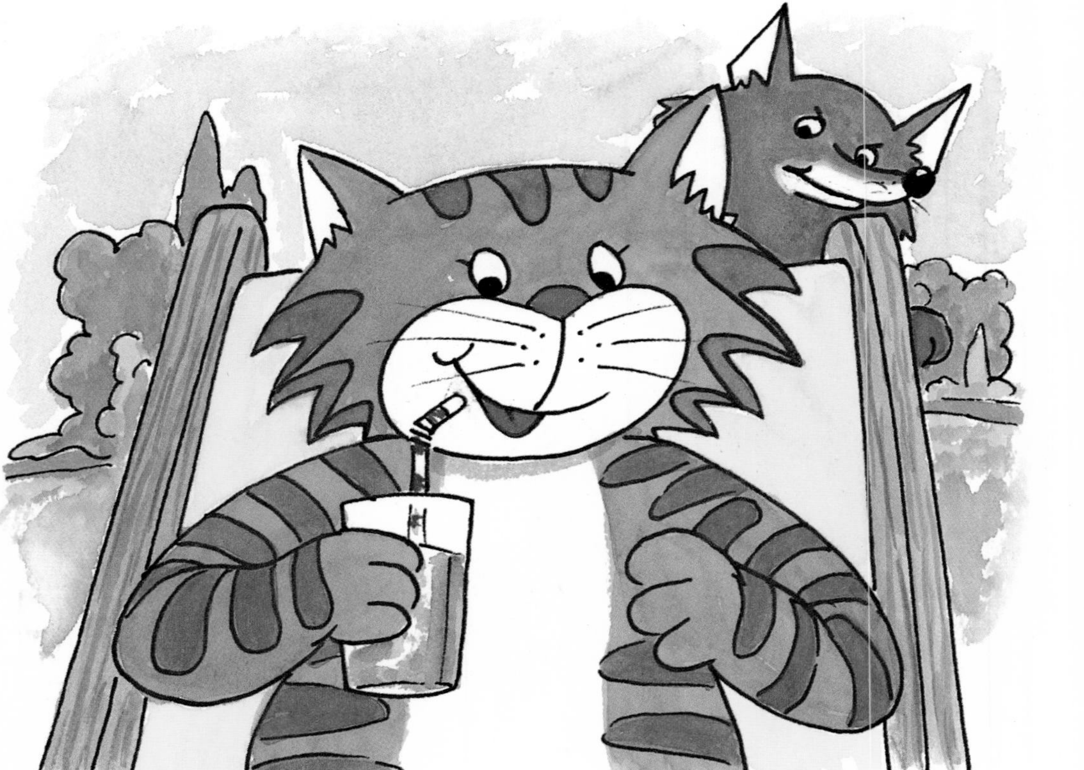

Jip is glad.

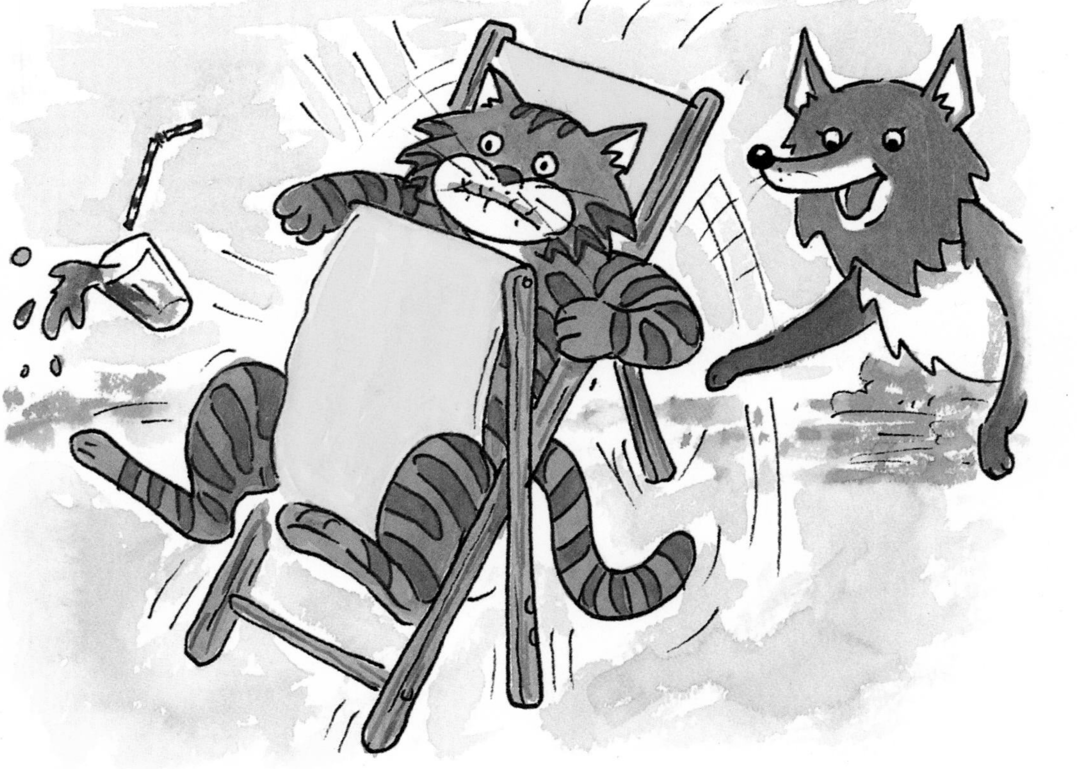

Sam is bad.

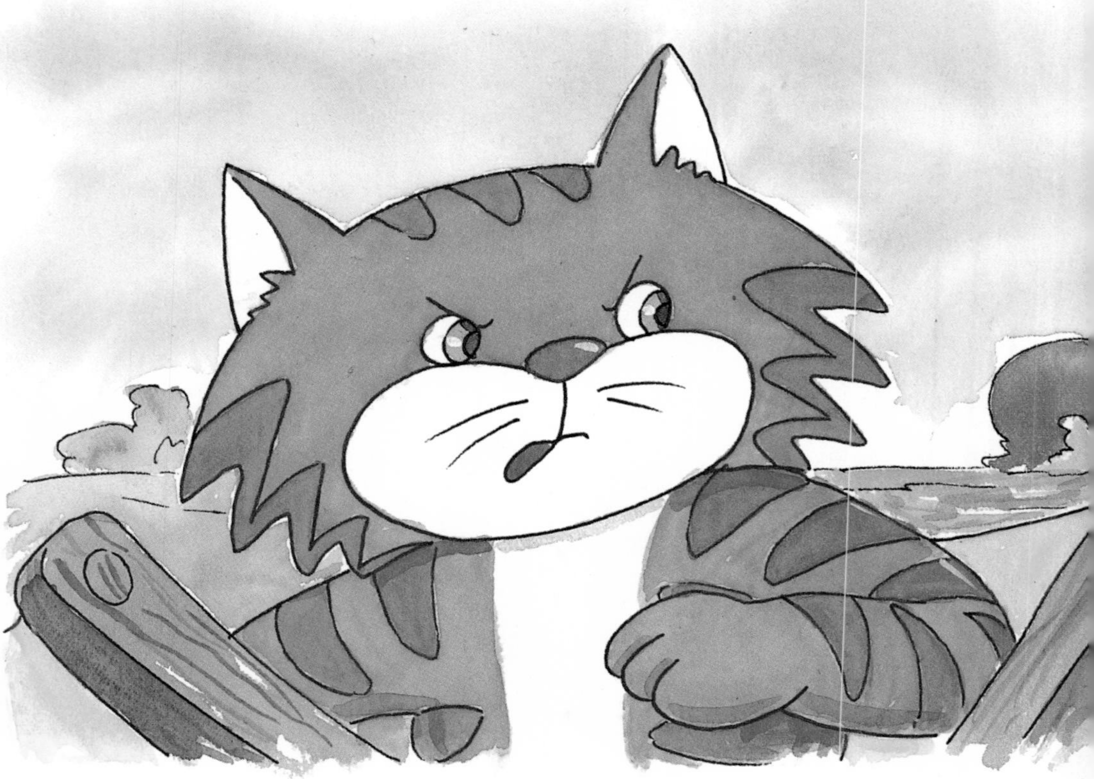

Jip is mad.

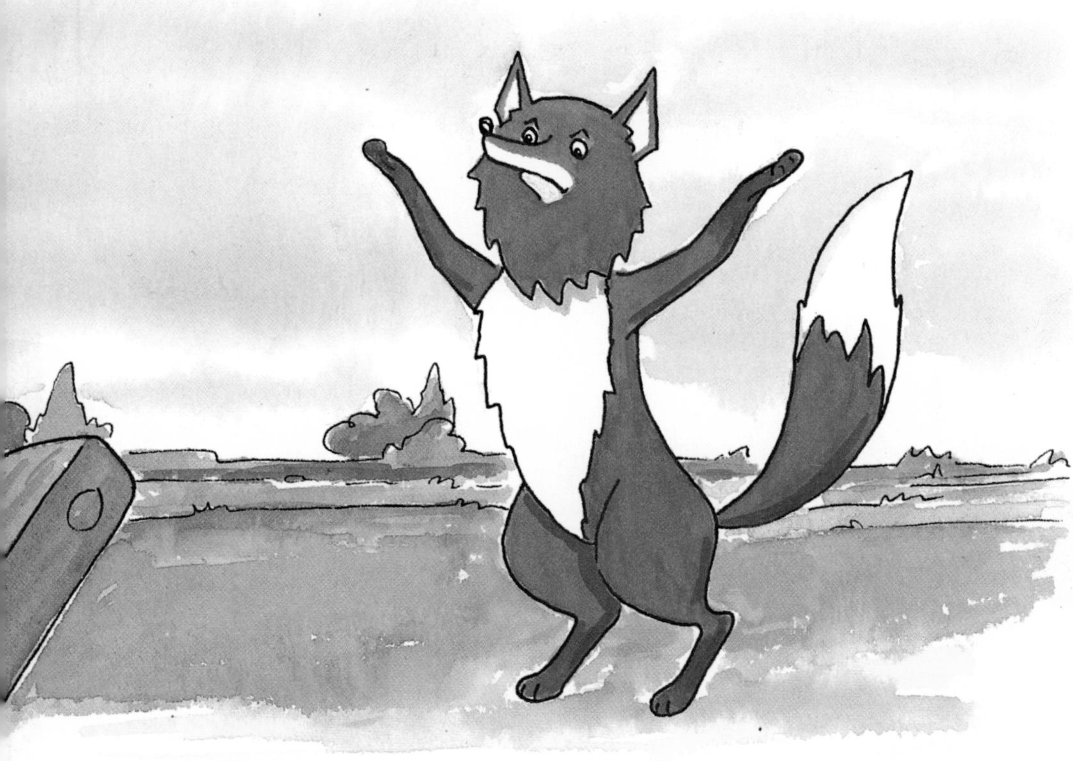

That's too bad.

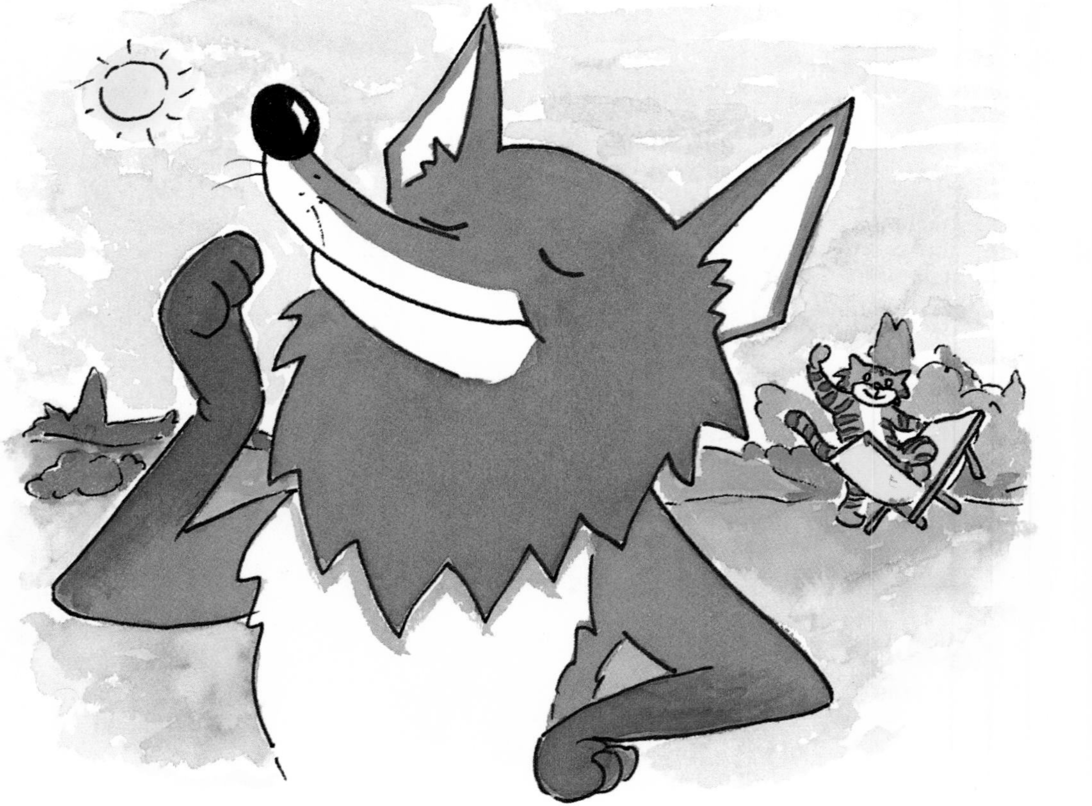

Sam is happy.

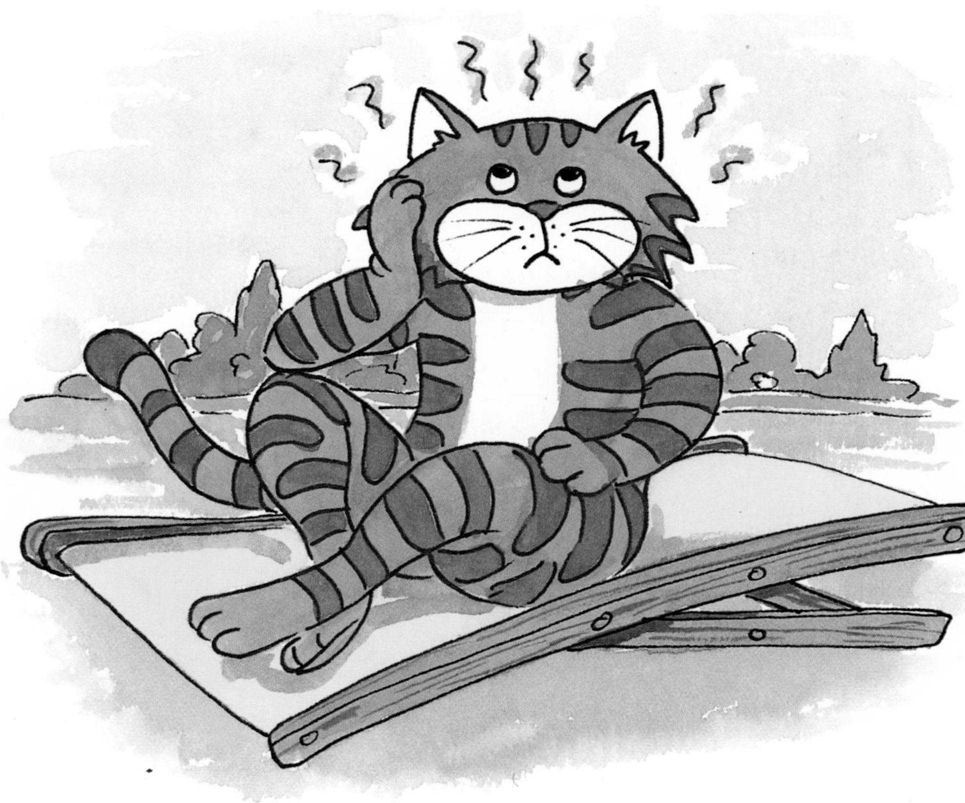

Jip is sad.

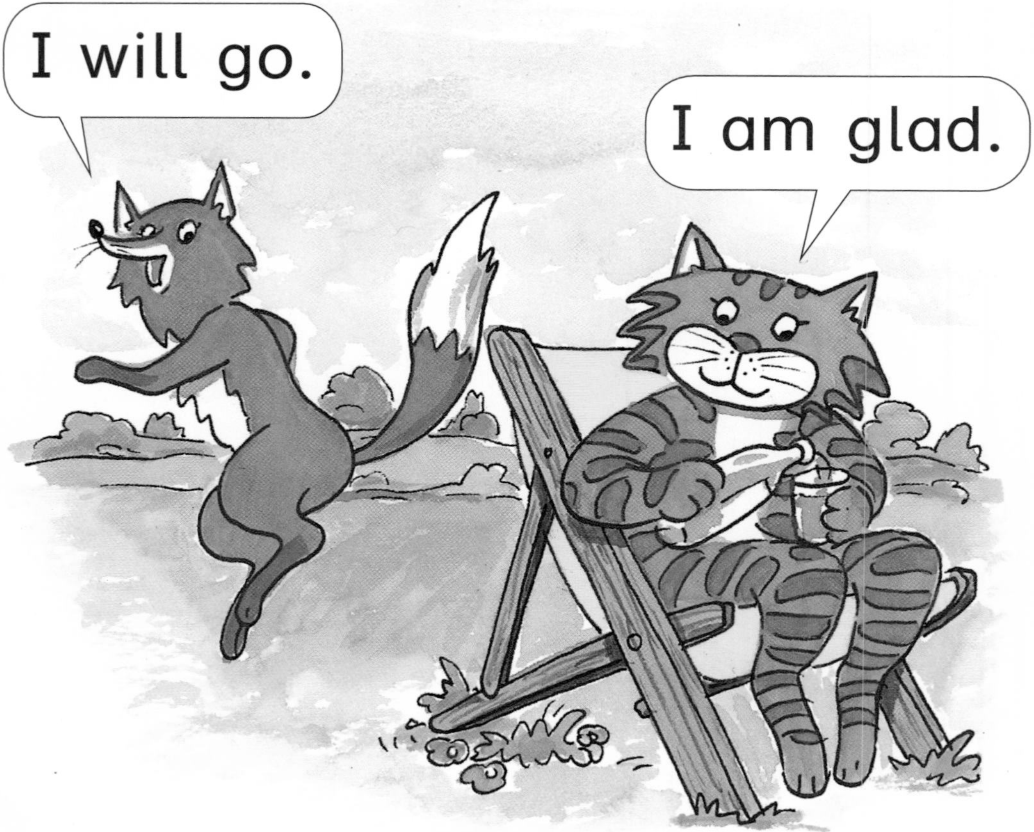
I will go.
I am glad.